I0441616

The month of May, from the illuminated manuscript
Les Très Riches Heures du duc de Berry

The Story of a Special Day
Volume 149

May
28

148th day of the year
(149th in leap years)
217 days remaining
until the end of the year.

by Michael Dobson

Timespinner
Press

Table of Contents

Cover: *The Spanish Armada Leaving the Port of Ferrol* by Sir Oswald W. Brierly — for the *Event of the Day.*

Back Cover and Frontispiece: The month of May, from the French Gothic illuminated manuscript *Les Très Riches Heures du duc de Berry.*

May 28 Quotations

You must believe me when I tell you that I have found it impossible to carry the heavy burden of responsibility and to discharge my duties as King as I would wish to do without the help and support of the woman I love.

> — *British monarch King Edward VIII, died May 28, 1972, abdication speech*

When you confront a problem, you begin to solve it.
> — *New York mayor Rudy Giuliani, born May 28, 1944*

The peak of the [Presidential] campaign happened in Albuquerque, where a local reporter said to me, "Dr. Commoner, are you a serious candidate or are you just running on the issues?"

> — *Environmentalist and third-party presidential candidate Barry Commoner, died May 28, 1917*

"I would like a medium Vodka dry Martini — with a slice of lemon peel. Shaken and not stirred, please."
> — *James Bond creator Ian Fleming, born May 28, 1908*

Every possible reezon that could ever be offered for altering the spelling of wurds, stil exists in full force; and if a gradual reform should not be made in our language, it wil proov that we are less under the influence of reezon than our ancestors.

> — *Lexicographer Noah Webster, died May 28, 1843, on reforming English spelling*

Event of the Day
The Spanish Armada Sets Sail

English ships and the Spanish Armada

The *Grande y Felicísima Armada* ("Great and Most Fortunate Navy") is known in English history as the Spanish Armada. The fleet, consisting of 151 ships manned by 8,000 sailors and 18,000 soldiers, set sail on May 28, 1588, for England. Its mission was to overthrow Elizabeth I of England and restore Catholic rule in that nation, as well as to stop English meddling in the Dutch Revolt against Spain.

Philip II, ruler of Spain and Portugal, had also been King of England during his marriage to Elizabeth's predecessor, Mary I, called "Bloody Mary" for her persecution of Protestants. He had already sponsored several plots to have Elizabeth overthrown and replaced by her cousin Mary Queen of Scots, but Elizabeth had her executed in 1587.

With the support of Pope Sixtus V, Philip II levied "crusade taxes" to build his fleet, and appointed an experienced commander, Álvaro de Bazán, to take charge of the invasion. Unfortunately, Bazán died before the fleet could be launched. His replacement, the Duke of Medina Sidonia was a courtier with no experience at sea.

The Spanish Armada took two full days for all ships to leave port. Their destination was the coast of Flanders, then part of the greater Netherlands, where 30,000 more soldiers under the command of the Duke of Parma were waiting to be carried across the Channel to invade England.

Bad weather hampered the Armada as it sailed up the coast. The English first sighted the Spanish fleet on July 19, but trapped by tide, were late getting to sea. By the night of July 20, the English fleet was able to tack upwind of the Armada, gaining the weather gage.

At the break of day on July 21, the two fleets clashed off the coast of Plymouth, England, near the Eddystone Rocks. The English fleet, commanded by Lord Howard of Effingham, with Sir Francis Drake as Vice Admiral, was larger than that of the Spanish but greatly inferior in firepower.

The first day's engagement was not decisive. The English fleet had superior speed and maneuverability, but their long range cannon fire was ineffective. That night, Sir Francis Drake managed to loot some of the damaged Spanish ships for gunpowder and gold, but in the darkness his fleet was scattered. It took a full day for the English to regroup, by which time the Armada had sailed closer to its destination.

On July 23 the fleets engaged in another indecisive engagement. Unable to gain shelter in only secure harbor within reach, the Armada made sail for Calais without waiting for Parma's army.

By July 27, the Armada reached Calais. Disease had whittled Parma's army from 30,000 to a mere 16,000, and worse, it would take at least six days for the transport-poor army to arrive.

The English, however, would not wait. At midnight on July 28, they sent eight fireships — warships filled with pitch and brimstone and set alight — downwind into the Spanish fleet. The Spanish scattered in disorganized confusion. The English closed in.

After the two earlier battles, the English had learned that they needed to close within 100 yards for their cannons to penetrate the oak hulls of the Spanish warships, but they were short of gunpowder. At the same time, they feared getting too close, because the Spanish would ensnare their ships with grappling hooks and board.

The culmination came at the Battle of Gravelines off the border of Flanders. The superior maneuverability of the English ships proved decisive. Again and again the English closed, firing cannon broadsides into the enemy ships. The battle raged for eight hours until the English, low on ammunition, were forced to disengage. Toward the end of the battle, some gunners were loading chains into their cannon.

The Spanish lost five ships. Worse, they were no longer in a position to rendezvous with the Duke of Parma. But they were still a formidable and dangerous foe, and the danger to the English was far from over.

The Armada withdrew to the north, pursued by the English even though they were nearly out of ammunition. By the time the two fleets neared the coast of Scotland, the English broke off the pursuit. Unable to complete his mission, the Duke of Medina Sedonia could only chart his course for home by the more hazardous route of traveling around Scotland and Ireland in the treacherous waters or the North Atlantic.

The ships were first pulled off course by the Gulf Stream current. Unable to measure longitude, the Armada turned south much farther to the west than they had planned. Ice and storms took more ships than had been lost to the English. Some 5,000 men perished; others were shipwrecked on the coast of Ireland, never to return home.

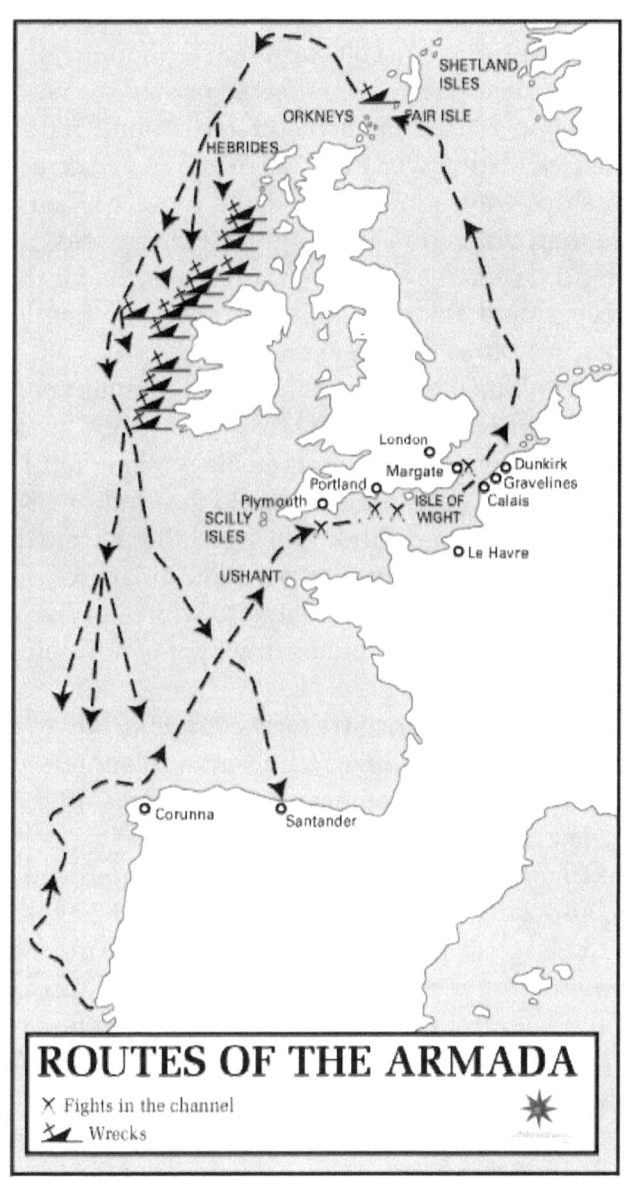

ROUTES OF THE ARMADA

X Fights in the channel
⚓ Wrecks

Only 67 ships of the original 151, and 10,000 men out of the original 26,000 survived, with many of the survivors near death from disease or starvation.

By contrast, the English suffered around 500 casualties, with fewer than 100 dead, and none of their ships were sunk. Disease and hunger killed more than did battle. The English treasury was nearly out of money; sailors waited months for their pay. Fearing the danger was not ended, the English were forced to keep a fleet on duty.

Queen Elizabeth I made her most famous speech following the defeat of the Armada, saying, "know I have the body of a weak and feeble woman; but I have the heart and stomach of a king – and of a King of England too, and think foul scorn that Parma or Spain, or any prince of Europe, should dare to invade the borders of my realm; to which, rather than any dishonour should grow by me, I myself will take up arms…"

The English victory was not complete, however. The following year, Elizabeth I sent a "Counter-Armada" the following year, and two more after that. The Spanish Navy kept control over its transatlantic routes. The undeclared Anglo-Spanish War, a sort of "Cold War" of its day, lasted 29 years.

The English victory over the Spanish Armada is often thought to be the moment that the balance of naval power in Europe shifted decisively in favor of the English. Advances in tactics, weaponry, and ship design, along with the boost to national pride engendered by that great victory, helped set Britain on the road to empire.

May 28 Holidays and Celebrations

Araw ng Watawat (Philippines)

Flag Day in the Philippines (*Araw ng Watawat*, or "Day of the Flag") is held on May 28 to commemorate its first use in the 1898 Battle of Alapan.

Armed Forces Day (Croatia)

Dan Oružanih snaga Republike Hrvatske (Armed Forces Day) in the Central European nation of Croatia is celebrated each year on May 28.

Derg Downfall Day (Ethiopia)

The Provisional Military Government of Socialist Ethiopia, known as the Derg, ruled Ethiopia from 1974 to 1987 following the ouster of Emperor ቀዳማዊ ኃይለ ሥላሴ (Haile Selassie I), imprisoning and executing tens of thousands without trial.

This triggered a long and bloody Ethiopian civil war along with widespread famine. The Derg junta was not fully removed until 1991, and its end is celebrated each May 28 as Ethiopia's National Day.

Republic Day (Armenia, Azerbaijan, Nepal)

On May 28, 1818, the countries of Armenia and Azerbaijan declared independence and officially became republics; Azerbaijan becoming the first democratic parliamentary republic in the Muslim world. Republic Day in both nations is celebrated on May 28.

In the nation of Nepal, elections following a revolution by the Communist Party of that country forced the monarch of Nepal to abdicate. Nepal officially became a federal democratic republic on May 28, 2008, now celebrated as their Republic Day.

Christian Feast Days

In **Western Christianity**, May 28 is the feast day of Bernard of Menthon, Germain of Paris, Lanfranc, Margaret Pole, and William of Gellone.

In **Eastern Orthodox Christianity**, May 28 is the feast of Saint Alexander, Bishop of Thessalonica; Saint Nicetas of Medikion; Saint Senator of Milan; Saint Justus of Urgell; Saint Gerontius of Moscow; and Saint Helen Manturova of Diveyevo; along with the Syntaxis of the Galich "Umilenie-Tenderness" Icon of the Mother of God. (These events are observed on June 10 by "Old Calendarists.")

What Happened on May 28?

585 BCE – **Battle of the Eclipse**

May 28, 585 BCE, is the earliest historical event whose date is known with certainty, and is the basis for which other dates in early history are calculated.

The Battle of the Eclipse (also known as the Battle of Halys) was the final engagement of a five-year war between the Lydians and the Medes in what is now Turkey. In the middle of the battle, according to the historian Herodotus, "suddenly the day became night." In other words, the umbral path of a solar eclipse passed over the battlefield.

Fearful of what they perceived as the wrath of the Gods, the combatants stopped fighting and negotiated a peace treaty. Because dates of solar eclipses can be calculated with great precision, we know the exact date of this battle.

1754 CE – **George Washington Starts a War**

On May 28, 1754, Lieutenant Colonel George Washington, leading a combined company of British Virginian colonial militia and Mingo Native American warriors ambushed a French Canadian force in what became known as the Battle of Jumonville Glen. Pursued by the French, Washington and his men were forced to capitulate at Fort Necessity.

The death of the French Canadian commander, claimed to be the result of an assassination ordered by Washington (historically controversial), triggered a series of escalations that helped start the Seven Years' War (also known as the French and Indian War) between Britain and France.

French artist's view of the Jumonville incident, showing the assassination of the French commander by English troops.

1830 CE – **Indian Removal Act Signed**

On May 28, 1830, US President Andrew Jackson signed the Indian Removal Act into law, which led to the forced relocation of Native Americans in the southern United States west of the Mississippi River in what became known as the "Trail of Tears." The "Five Civilized Tribes" of Cherokee, Chickasaw, Choctaw, Muscogee-Creek, and Seminole were all affected. While the act was very popular in the South, it was opposed by numerous missionaries and by future president Abraham Lincoln.

1905 CE – **Battle of Tsushima**

The only decisive sea battle fought by modern steel battleship fleets, the Battle of Tsushima, the major engagement of the Russo-Japanese War, took place May 27-28, 1905, resulting in a decisive Japanese victory. The battle was also notable as the first in which wireless telegraphy played a role, making it the beginning of electronic warfare.

1934 CE – **Dionne Quintuplets Born**

On May 28, 1934, Elizire Dionne, who had five previous children, gave birth to the first known quintuplets to survive infancy. The Canadian government passsed legislation to make the quintuplets wards of the Crown and turned them into a major tourist draw for Ontario, known as "Quintland," with over 3 million visitors between 1936 and 1943. As of 2013, three of the Dionne quintuplets are still alive.

Ontario Premier Mitchell Hepburn with the Dionne quintuplets

1937 CE – **Volkswagen Founded**

The Volkswagen company was founded on May 28, 1937. Pressed by the Nazi government, its job was to produce a low-end basic car available to the mass market. Adapting a design by Ferdinand Porsche into the iconic "beetle" known today, the new company produced only a few cars before the end of the war.

Following World War II, a British officer saw the potential in the inexpensive vehicle and persuaded the British government to order 20,000 of them. Attempts to sell the company to British, French, and American companies failed, and Volkswagen continued to produce cars on its own.

A sculpture built from Volkswagens, Karlsruhe, Germany
(Photo: Michael Kaufffman)

1937 CE – **Recapture of Narvik**

On May 28, 1937, Allied troops captured the strategic
Norwegian town of Narvik in the first major Allied
land victory of World War II. Narvik was
distinguished by an ice-free harbor allowing the
shipment of iron ore, an important resource.

1952 CE – **Greek Women Get the Right to Vote**

On May 28, 1952, the right to vote was extended to
women in Greece. Women's rights received a setback
under the military rule from 1967 to 1974, when the
government instituted dress codes and other
requirements for subservience on the part of women.

1964 CE – **Palestine Liberation Organization Founded**

The PLO, or Palestine Liberation Organization (منظمة التحرير الفلسطينية), was founded on May 28, 1964, as an outgrowth of the 1964 Arab League summit in Cairo. It was designated as a terrorist organization by the United States in 1987, and the organization carried out a number of attacks, ranging from the 970 Avivim school bus massacre, the Munich massacre of Israeli Olympic athletes, and the Coastal Road massacre.

In 1993, the PLO officially recognized Israel's right to exist and renounced violence and terrorism. Today it is recognized by the United Nations and over 100 states (including Israel) as the "sole legitimate representative of the Palestinian people."

1987 CE – **Mathias Rust Lands in Red Square**

On May 28, 1987, a 19-year old West German pilot named Mathias Rust flew from Finland to Moscow without authorization, landing in Red Square. He was jailed for a little more than a year.

Rust's flight, according to a former director of the US National Security Agency, irreparably damaged the reputation of the Soviet military, allowing Soviet leader Mikhail Gorbachev to remove numerous military officers opposed to his reforms, and is thus credited with helping to bring an end to the Cold War.

1998 CE – **Pakistan Becomes a Nuclear Power**

On May 28, 1998, in response to a series of nuclear tests by India, Pakistan conducted five public nuclear tests blasts in what was code named Chagai-I. This made Pakistan the seventh nuclear armed power in the world, in spite of widespread international condemnation of both the Indian and Pakistani tests.

1999 CE – *The Last Supper* **Returns to Display**

After 21 years of painstaking restoration work, Leonardo da Vinci's masterpiece *The Last Supper* was returned to public display on May 28, 1999. Visitors must book ahead to view the painting, located in the Convent of Santa Maria della Grazie in Milan, Italy.

Photographs of Leonardo da Vinci's *The Last Supper* taken before
(above) and after (below) its restoration.

Who Was Born on May 28?

Arts and Literature

Lynn Johnston (May 28, 1947 —)

Lynn Johnson is known for her long-running comic strip *For Better or For Worse*.

Promotional image of Lynn Johnston's *For Better or For Worse*

Maeve Binchy (May 28, 1940 — July 30, 2012)

Irish novelist and playwright Maeve Binchy's many honors include the British Book Award for Lifetime Achievement, the Irish PEN Award, and others. Her novels *Circle of Friends, Tara Road*, and *How About You* were made into films.

Roger Fisher (May 28, 1922 — August 25, 2012)

Harvard Law School professor Roger Fisher was director of the Harvard Negotiation Project and co-author of the 1981 best-seller *Getting to YES: Negotiating Agreement Without Giving In* with William Ury.

Walker Percy (May 28, 1916 — May 10, 1990)

American Southern author Walker Percy is known for his novels set in and around New Orleans. His 1961 novel *The Moviegoer* won the US National Book Award for Fiction.

Patrick White (May 28, 1912 — September 30, 1990)

Patrick White is the only Australian to have received the Nobel Prize for Literature. His 1973 novel *The Eye of the Storm* was adapted into a 2011 film.

Ian Fleming (May 28, 1908 — August 12, 1964)

British Naval Intelligence officer and former journalist Ian Fleming created the fictional spy James Bond, writing twelve novels and two short story collections about the character that sold over 100 million copies worldwide. Over 25 films have featured the James Bond character.

For Your Eyes Only (Ian Fleming), by Constance Vlahoulis

Crime

Santo Trafficante, Sr. (May 28, 1886 — August 11, 1954)

Sicilian-born mobster Santo Trafficante built the Tampa Mafia, the only original Mafia crime family in Florida. His son Santo Trafficante, Jr., took over the syndicate, and worked with the CIA on the assassination attempts against Fidel Castro.

Film, Television, and Theatre

Elisabeth Hasselbeck (May 28, 1977 —)

Television personality Hasselbeck is known as a finalist on *Survivor* and as a co-host of the talk show *The View*.

Alicia Minshew (May 28, 1974 —)

Minshew played Kendall Hart on the soap opera *All My Children*.

Justin Kirk (May 28, 1969 —)

Kirk is best known for playing Andy Botwin in the Showtime series *Weeds*.

Christa Miller (May 28, 1964 —)

Christa Miller had major roles in the TV series *The Drew Carey Show, Scrubs*, and *Cougar Town*.

Brandon Cruz (May 28, 1962 —)

Cruz is best known as a child actor who played Eddie Corbett in the TV sitcom *The Courtship of Eddie's Father.*

Sondra Locke (May 28, 1944 or 1947 —)

Actress Sondra Locke received an Academy Award nomination for *The Heart is a Lonely Hunter.* She appeared in numerous films with her then-partner Clint Eastwood, including *The Outlaw Josey Wales, The Gauntlet,* and *Every Which Way But Loose.*

Patricia Quinn (May 28, 1944 —)

Known primarily for her role as Magenta in *The Rocky Horror Picture Show*, Quinn appeared in numerous other film and television roles.

Beth Howland (May 28, 1941 —)

Stage and film actress Beth Howland is best known for her role as Vera in the TV sitcom *Alice.*

Carroll Baker (May 28, 1931 —)

Dramatic actress and sex symbol Carroll Baker's films include *Baby Doll, Giant, The Big Country,* and *Harlow.* She won a Golden Globe and was nominated for another Golden Globe and an Oscar.

Carroll Baker

Johnny Wayne (May 28, 1918 — July 18, 1990)

Canadian comedian Johnny Wayne is best known as part of the comedy duo Wayne and Shuster.

Thora Hird (May 28, 1911 — March 15, 2003)

Thora Hird won two BAFTA Best Actress Awards and appeared in numerous British films and television series.

Dame Thora Hird

Rachel Kempson (May 28, 1910— May 24, 2003)

English actress Rachel Kempson appeared in such films as *Tom Jones, Georgy Girl*, and *Out of Africa*. She is perhaps best known as the wife of actor Sir Michael Redgrave and the mother of actresses Vanessa and Lynn Redgrave.

Tony Pastor (May 28, 1837 — August 26, 1908)

Impressario and theatre owner Tony Pastor is considered the "Father of Vaudeville" for developing family oriented variety shows.

Government, Politics and Military

Marco Rubio (May 28, 1971 —)

Florida senator Marco Rubio has been called the "crown prince of the Tea Party movement."

Rudy Giuliani (May 28, 1944 —)

Rudy Giuliani served two terms as Mayor of New York City. He was named *Time* Magazine's Person of the Year in 2001 for his response to the 9/11 attacks.

Betty Shabazz (May 28, 1934 — June 23, 1997)

Wife of murdered civil rights activist Malcolm X, Betty Shabazz became Director of Institutional Advancement and Public Affairs at Medgar Evers College and served in numerous advisory roles.

Barry Commoner (May 28, 1917 — September 30, 2012)

Ecologist and environmentalist Barry Commoner ran for the US presidency on the 1980 Citizens Party ticket and served as editor of *Science Illustrated* magazine.

Sepp Dietrich (May 28, 1892 — April 21, 1966)

Nazi general Josef "Sepp" Dietrich, a World War I sergeant, began as Adolf Hitler's chauffeur, and through personal loyalty advanced to the rank of SS-Oberst-Gruppenführer, a four-star rank. He led the 6th Panzer Army, the leading force in the Battle of the Bulge. He was convicted in the Nürnberg trials for his involvement in the Malmedy massacre of US prisoners of war and for his role in the "Night of the Long Knives" in 1934. He served ten years in prison.

P. G. T. Beauregard (May 28, 1818 — February 20, 1893)

The first prominent Confederate general of the American Civil War, Beauregard commanded the defenses of Charleston at Fort Sumter, won the First Battle of Bull Run, and saved Petersburg, Virginia from overwhelmingly superior Union Army forces.

William Pitt the Younger (May 28, 1759 — January 23, 1806)

Following in the footsteps of his father, William Pitt the Elder, Pitt the Younger became Britain's youngest prime minister at the age of 24. He led Britain through the Napoleonic Wars, and helped rehabilitate the country's finances following the loss of the American colonies to revolution.

Joseph-Ignace Guillotin (May 28, 1738 — March 26, 1814)

Although Joseph-Ignace Guillotin did not invent the guillotine (actually invented by Antoine Louis), he was the first to propose "a machine that beheads painlessly," and thus gave his name to the device based on his idea. Although a person named Guillotin was later executed by guillotine, Joseph-Ignace died of natural causes.

King George I of Great Britain (May 28, 1660 — June 11, 1714)

Although there were some fifty Roman Catholic relatives with closer blood relationships to Queen Anne, only a Protestant was eligible to ascend the throne. Following her death, her German Protestant second cousin George, Elector of Hanover, became King George I of Great Britain and Ireland, ending the House of Stuart and beginning the House of Hanover, which lasted until the death of Queen Victoria in 1901.

Music

Kylie Minogue (May 28, 1968 —)

Australian singer and actress Kylie Minogue hits include "I Should Be So Lucky," "Spinning Around," and "Can't Get You Out of My Head."

King George I of Great Britain, portrait by Sir Godfrey Kneller, Bt.

Phil Vassar (May 28, 1964 —)

Named 1999 Country Songwriter of the Year, Phil Vassar became a recording artist in 2000, and has charted 19 singles, including two Number #1 hits, on the country charts.

Wendy O. Williams (May 28, 1949 — April 6, 1998)

Wendy O. Williams was known as the "Queen of Shock Rock" for her stage theatrics as lead singer of the punk band The Plasmatics. She received a Grammy nomination in 1985.

John Fogerty (Photo: Brennan Schnell)

John Fogerty (May 28, 1945 —)

John Fogerty is best known as lead singer-songwriter of Creedence Clearwater Revival. His hits include "Proud Mary," "Born on the Bayou," "Bad Moon Rising," "Down on the Corner," and "Lookin' Out My Back Door."

Gary Stewart (May 28, 1944 — December 15, 2003)

Country artist Gary Stewart's biggest hit was 1975's "She's Actin' Single (I'm Drinkin' Doubles)." *Time* Magazine named him "king of honkytonk."

Gladys Knight (May 28, 1944 —)

Known as the "Empress of Soul," Gladys Knight is best known for her hits with the group Gladys Knight & the Pips. She has received seven Grammy awards.

Prince Buster (May 28, 1938 —)

Jamaican singer-songwriter Cecil Bustamente Campbell, better known as Prince Buster, is a key figure in the history of ska and rocksteady, influencing the course of Jamaican contemporary music.

Papa John Creach (May 28, 1917 — February 22, 1994)

Blues violinist Papa John Creach played for Jefferson Airplane, Jefferson Starship, and Hot Tuna.

T-Bone Walker (May 28, 1910 — March 16, 1975)

Aaron T. Walker, best known by his stage name, was a pioneer of the jump blues and electric blues sound, and was listed by *Rolling Stone* magazine as one of the 100 greatest guitarists of all time. He is a member of the Blues Hall of Fame and the Rock and Roll Hall of Fame.

T-Bone Walker (Photo: Heinrich Klaffs)

Science and Medicine

Patch Adams (May 28, 1945 —)

Physician Patch Adams founded the Gesundheit! Institute, whose members dress as clowns for the entertainment of hospital patients, orphans, and others. The 1998 film *Patch Adams*, starring Robin Williams, was based on him.

Ruby Payne-Scott (May 28, 1912 — May 25, 1981)

Australian physicist and astronomer Ruby Payne-Scott was one of the first people in the world to consider the possibility of radio astronomy, and the first female radio astronomer.

Sports

Craig Kimbrel (May 28, 1988 —)

Atlanta Braves pitcher Kimbrel received the 2011 National League Rookie of the Year Award.

Alexei Nemov (Алексей Немов) (May 28, 1976 —)

Russian gymnast Nemov has won 12 Olympic medals, including four gold.

Ekaterina Gordeeva (Екатерина Гордеева) (May 28, 1971 —)

Figure skater Gordeeva won gold along with her husband and partner Sergei Grinkov in the 1988 and 1994 Olympic games.

Glen Rice (May 28, 1967 —)

Basketball small forward Glen Rice ranks 11th in NBA history with 1,559 three-point field goals in his 15 year professional career.

Jeff Fenech (May 28, 1964 —)

Boxer Jeff Fenech won world championships in the Bantamweight, Super Bantamweight, and Featherweight categories. He was inducted into the International Boxing Hall of Fame in 2002.

Mark Howe (May 28, 1955 —)

Ice hockey defenceman Mark Howe played 16 seasons in the National Hockey League and six seasons in the World Hockey Association. He is a member of the Hockey Hall of Fame.

Jerry West (May 28, 1938 —)

Known as "Mr. Clutch," Los Angeles Lakers guard Jerry West was voted into the Naismith Basketball Hall of Fame in 1980 and voted one of the 50 Greatest Players in NBA History in 1996.

Red Horner (May 28, 1909 — April 27, 2005)

Toronto Maple Leafs defenceman Red Horner was inducted into the Hockey Hall of Fame in 1965.

Jim Thorpe (May 28, 1888 — March 28, 1953)

Voted the Greatest Athlete of the Twentieth Century in a poll of sports fans, Jim Thorpe (left) won Olympic gold medals in pentathlon and decathlon, and played collegiate and professional football, professional basketball, and professional baseball. Of combined Native American and European ancestry, he was known in the Sauk language as Wa-Tho-Huk, or "Bright Path.

Who Died on May 28?

Film and Television

Gary Coleman (February 8, 1968 — May 28, 2010)

Coleman was best known as a child actor in the sitcom *Diff'rent Strokes*.

Phil Hartman (September 24, 1948 — May 28, 1998)

Canadian-American comedian Phil Hartman was best known as a cast member of *Saturday Night Live*. He wrote the screenplay for the film *Pee-wee's Big Adventure* and starred in the NBC sitcom *News Radio*.

Eric Morecambe (May 14, 1926 — May 28, 1984)

English comedian Eric Morecambe was known as half of the comedy duo Morecambe and Wise.

Arthur Brough (February 26, 1905 — May 28, 1978)

British actor Arthur Brough played salesman Ernest Grainger on the BBC sitcom *Are You Being Served?*

Letters

Mildred Benson (July 10, 1905 — May 28, 2002)

Children's book author Mildred Benson wrote or contributed to 23 of the first 30 original *Nancy Drew* mysteries, writing under the Stratemeyer Syndicate pen name "Carolyn Keene."

Anne Brontë (January 17, 1820 — May 28, 1849)

Youngest member of the Brontë literary family, Anne Brontë was a poet and novelist. Less famous than her sisters Charlotte *(Jane Eyre)* and Emily *(Wuthering Heights)*, she is known for her two novels, *Agnes Grey* and *The Tenant of Wildfell Hall.*

Noah Webster (October 16, 1758 — May 28, 1843)

Lexicographer Noah Webster is considered the "father of American scholarship and education." His name is associated with American dictionaries, having published the first such dictionary in 1828.

Military

Audie Murphy (June 20, 1925 — May 28, 1971)

One of the most decorated American combat soldiers of the Second World War, Audie Murphy received the Medal of Honor among other awards for heroism. Following the war, he played himself in the autobiographical 1955 film *To Hell and Back,* and went on to act in 44 films and a television series, *Whispering Smith*.

Audie Murphy in *The Red Badge of Courage*

Music

Leopold Mozart (November 14, 1719 — May 28, 1787)

Violinist and music teacher Leopold Mozart is best known as the father of Wolfgang Amadeus Mozart.

Politics and Government

Edward VIII of Great Britain (June 23, 1894 — May 28, 1972)

Eldest son and heir of King George V, Edward VIII abdicated the throne after 326 days as monarch to marry divorced American socialite Wallis Simpson, becoming Duke of Windsor. His younger brother Albert ascended the throne as George VI.

Carter Glass (January 4, 1858 — May 28, 1946)

Newspaper publisher and congressman Carter Glass gave his name to the 1913 Glass-Owen Act that created the Federal Reserve System and the 1933 Glass-Steagall Act that separated investment and commercial banking and established the FDIC.

Henry Dundas, 1st Viscount Melville (April 28, 1742 — May 28, 1811)

During his political career, Henry Dundas had almost total control of Scottish politics, nicknamed the "uncrowned King of Scotland." He was the last government official to be impeached in the United Kingdom and is the subject of one of the most prominent memorials in Edinburgh.

Religion

Wulfstan (Unknown — May 28, 1023)

Bishop of London and Worcester and Archbishop of York, Wulfstan drafted law codes for English monarchs Æthelred the Unready and Cnut the Great, and is considered one of the two major writers of the late Anglo-Saxon period.

Science and Medicine

Alfred Adler (February 7, 1870 — May 28, 1937)

Alfred Adler developed the school of individual psychology, emphasizing the inferiority complex and the importance of the social element in the readjustment process of the individual.

Sports

Julius Boros (March 3, 1920 — May 28, 1994)

Golfer Julius Boros was elected to the World Golf Hall of Fame in 1982.

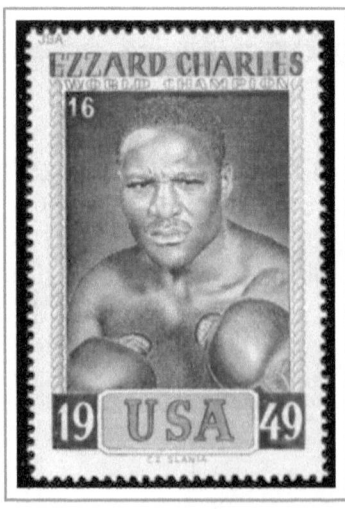

Ezzard Charles
(July 7, 1921 — May 28, 1975)

Boxer Ezzard Charles was World Heavyweight Champion from 1949 to 1951. He is a member of the International Boxing Hall of Fame.

May
The Fifth Month

"Then came fair May, the fairest maid on ground,
Deck'd all with dainties of the season's pride,
And throwing flowers out of her lap around. ."

　　　　— *Edward Spenser,* The Faerie Queene, *Book VII*

According to many scholars, the month of May takes its name from the Roman goddess Maia, an earth goddess who was the mother of Mercury. The poet Ovid, on the other hand, claimed that May took its name from the Latin *maiores*, meaning ancestors. In either case, the month of May in ancient Rome was marked by sacrifices to Maia, and her son Mercury was honored on the Ides of May (May 15).

May is the fifth month of the year in both Julian and Gregorian calendars. It was originally the third month in ancient Rome, because the new year began on March 1. Although Julius Caesar changed the length of several months during his great calendar reform (the Julian calendar), the length of May has remained constant at 31 days.

In the northern hemisphere, May occurs in the springtime, and in the southern hemisphere, May takes place in fall. Strangely, no other month begins or ends on the same day of the week as the beginning or ending of May, although January of the following year always begins and ends on the same day of the week as this year's May.

May in Other Cultures

In Latin and Old English, the month of May was named *Maius*, and it is *Mai* in French. In Arabic, the month is مايو, pronounced *māyū*. In Chinese, the equivalent month is 五月. Croatians call the month

svibanj and in Czech it is *květen*. In Finland, it is *toukokuu*. The Jewish month of Sivan (סִיוָן) normally falls in May-June. It is the third month of the Jewish ecclesiastical year. The Irish called the month *bealtaine*, and it marked the beginning of summer. Slovenians call May *veliki traven*, or the month of the big grass.

May Superstitions

- May is an unlucky month for getting married.

- Never buy a broom in May.

- "Wash a blanket in May / Wash a dear one away."

- Cats born in May will bring snakes into the house.

- "Those who bathe in May / Will soon be laid in clay."

May Symbols

Birthstone: Emerald

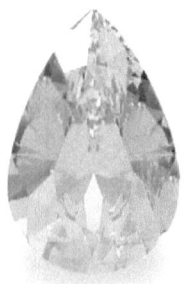

Birth Flowers: Lily of the Valley and Hawthorn.

Lily of the Valley

Common Hawthorn

The month of May, by Simon Bening

May Events

Honorary Months

Presidents, Congresses, and nations around the world issue proclamations recognizing particular months to honor certain causes. These events generally fall in April. (All US unless otherwise noted.)

- American Bike Month
- Asian Pacific American Heritage Month
- Asparagus Month
- Drinking Water Month
- Jewish American Heritage Month
- Mental Heath Awareness Month
- Music Month (New Zealand)
- National ALS Awareness Month
- National Brain Tumor Awareness Month
- National Military Appreciation Month
- National Moving Month
- National Smile Month (United Kingdom)
- Older Americans Month
- Skin Cancer Awareness Month
- South Asian Heritage Month

Moveable and Multi-Day Events

Some events take place over a specific week or time period. Start and finish dates may vary from year to year. Some events occur on different days each year (such as "fourth Saturday of a month").

Children's Day (Hungary)

The last Sunday in May is Children's Day in Hungary.

Indianapolis 500 (Indianapolis, Indiana)

Known as the "Greatest Spectacle in Racing" and one of the three most prestigious motor racing events in the world, the Indianapolis 500 is held each year on the Sunday preceding Memorial Day.

International Headband Week (Worldwide)

During International Headband Week, which runs from Monday through Friday in the last week of May, people are encouraged to wear headbands to work and to other social events to promote confidence and character building.

Memorial Day (United States)

Memorial Day in the United States is a federal holiday that occurs each year on the last Monday in May. It honors the men and women who have died while serving in the United States Armed Forces.

Originally, it was known as Decoration Day, established following the American Civil War to honor Union and Confederate soldiers who died in the conflict. It expanded to cover all Americans who died in military service.

On Memorial Day, volunteers place American flags on each grave in national cemeteries and people visit the graves of relatives who died performing military service, often picnicking there. A National Memorial Day Concert is held on the west lawn of the US Capitol, and parades are held in many cities.

Memorial Day also serves as the unofficial beginning of summer. Following the 1968 passage of the Uniform Monday Holiday Act, Memorial Day moved from its traditional date of May 30 to its current date of the last Monday, creating a long weekend.

Mother's Day (Algeria, Dominican Republic, France, Haiti, Mauritius, Morocco, Sweden, Tunisia)

The last Sunday in May is Mother's Day in numerous countries.

Vesākha (वैशाख)

The Buddhist holiday day known as Vesākha or simply Vesak commemorates the birth, enlightenment, and death of Gautama Buddha. It is celebrated on the first full moon of the month of Vesākha, which normally falls in April or May, and in leap years in the month of June.

"On Decoration Day," cartoon by John T. McCutcheon, 1906

May Zodiac Signs

From the perspective of someone on Earth, the Sun appears to move through the sky throughout the year, along a path astronomers call the ecliptic plane. The ecliptic plane is divided into twelve constellations, known as the zodiac, based on traditionally observed patterns of stars. On your birthday, you can't see your constellation, because it's part of the daytime sky.

The zodiac was first developed by Babylonian astronomers about 2,500 years ago. Because they were unaware that the Earth wobbles like a spinning top (a motion known as *precession*), they didn't make allowance for the fact that the Sun's path through the zodiac changes over time.

That means there are now two sets of dates for your birth sign. The *tropical* dates are the original Babylonian dates; the *siderial* dates tell you where the Sun actually appears as it moves along its annual path.

In tropical reckoning, May 28 is in Gemini, and in siderial reckoning, May 28 is in Taurus.

Gemini

Tropical May 22 to June 21

Siderial June 16 to July 15

In Greek and Roman mythology, Castor and Pollux were twin brothers, both born to Leda. Castor, however, was a mortal, son of the King of Sparta, whereas Pollux was the son of Zeus, who had seduced (or raped) Leda while disguised as a swan. When Castor was killed, Pollux asked to share his divine immortality with his brother, and so Zeus transformed them both into the constellation of Gemini.

In astrology, Gemini is considered a masculine and air sign, ruled by Mercury. Geminis are supposed to be flexible, responsive, and sociable. Positive traits include intelligence and independence; negative traits include impatience and impulsiveness.

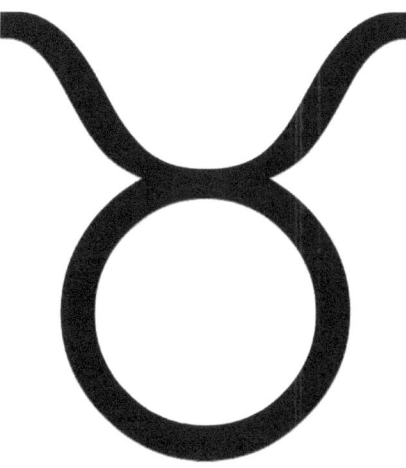

Taurus

Tropical April 21 to May 21

Siderial May 16 to June 15

In Greek mythology, Taurus was a disguise adopted by Zeus, who appeared to the maiden Europa in the form of a gentle white bull. Europa unwisely got too close, and Zeus kidnapped her to the island of Crete, where she bore him three sons, including Minos, builder of the labyrinth that housed the minotaur.

In astrology, Taurus is an earth sign, and Taureans are supposed to be quiet, gentle, compassionate, and stubborn. Taureans can appreciate the finer things in life and are cautious with money.

Illustration by Edward Penfield

What Day of the Week is May 28?

On what day of the week does May 28 fall?

Surprisingly, this isn't an easy question. Because the calendar year is 365 days long (366 in leap years), it doesn't divide evenly by the seven days of the week.

Also, the Earth goes around the Sun in about 365-1/4 days, so a calendar tends to drift over time. That's why the same date falls on different weekdays in different years.

This is made even more complicated by a change in calendars that took place in 1582. Our modern calendar has its roots in ancient Rome, in a calendar reform conducted by Julius Caesar. Caesar commissioned mathematicians to attack the problem, and they came up with the idea of *leap years*, and thus standardized the calendar for centuries to come. This was called the *Julian calendar.*

Over time, however, the small errors in Caesar's calculation compounded. That's why Pope Gregory XIII commissioned the *Gregorian calendar*, used in most of the world today. Some countries converted in 1582, when the calendar was first developed; some converted later; other still haven't changed.

Gregorian and Julian aren't the only types of calendars. The Hebrew year, the Islamic year, and many other calendars are used in different parts of the world and among different people.

You can convert Gregorian dates to other calendars, including the Hebrew calendar, the Islamic calendar, and even the Mayan calendar by visiting the Fourmilab Calendar Converter at http://www.fourmilab.ch/documents/calendar/.

Chinese calendar systems are quite complex and have changed several times; a full discussion is far beyond the scope of this book. If you're interested, you can find information here: http://www.hermetic.ch/cal_stud/chinese_cal.htm.

A 50-year brass perpetual calendar.

Copyright, Credit, and Contact

Follow Us

Our blog *Dobson's Improbable History* (http://
improbhistory.blogspot.com) features short articles
on events and people associated with each day, and
updates several times each week. You can also get a
daily "What Happened In History" message and all
the latest Timespinner Press news by following us on
Facebook at https://www.facebook.com/
TimespinnerPress. Our Twitter feed
@SidewiseThinker links you to all our News of the
Day.

Contact Us

Find an error or a format problem? Want information
about the series, about us, or about when the volume
for your special day might be available? Please email
us at editor@timespinnerpress.com. (We also take
requests if your special day isn't yet complete. Please
give us at least six weeks' notice if possible.)

On Dates

Historians use "CE" (Common Era) and
"BCE" (Before the Common Era) instead of the more
common "AD" (*Anno Domini*, or Year of Our Lord)
and "BC" (Before Christ), reflecting the fact that the
year-numbering system established by the Gregorian
calendar is used throughout the world in many
countries not culturally Christian.

The CE/BCE designation dates back to at least
1708, and has been adopted as a standard by the
United Nations and the Universal Postal Union.
Because this series of books covers events and
people of all nations and cultures, we use the CE/
BCE terms.

The abbreviation "O.S." on some dates refers to
the fact that the Russian Empire did not switch from
the Julian to the Gregorian calendar at the same time
as the rest of Europe, and therefore some figures and
events have two dates. (See "What Day of the
Week…" for an explanation of Julian and Gregorian
dates.)

People and events whose original names are not
in the Western alphabet have their native names
(where possible) in the appropriate script shown in
parenthesis. If you are using an e-reader to access an
electronic version of this book, all characters don't
always display on all devices.

Sources and Art Credits

We owe a great debt to Wikipedia, which is our first stop for research. We attempt to make independent confirmation of all important dates and facts through a variety of other sources. Other sources we frequently use include the Library of Congress; "on this day" listings from *Encyclopedia Britannica*, the New York *Times*, and the BBC; and, of course, the always essential Google.

All art and photographs are either in the public domain, used under a Creative Commons license, or with a "fair use" justification, and most frequently come from Wikimedia Commons and the Library of Congress Prints and Photographs Division.

Attribution is provided where requested by the copyright owner or when of historical significance, listed below. For information about any particular illustration or photograph, please contact us.

- The cover painting, *The Spanish Armada Leaving the Port of Ferrol* by Sir Oswald W. Brierly is from the 19th century, and can be found in Britain's National Maritime Museum. It is in the public domain because its copyright has expired.

- The illustration of the month of May used on the back cover and as the frontispiece is from the French Gothic illuminated manuscript *Les Très Riches Heures du duc de Berry* by the Limbourg Brothers, Jean Colombe, and an intermediate painter whose name is lost to history. It is in the public domain because its copyright has expired.

- The painting of English ships and the Spanish Armada was painted in the 16th century by an artist whose name is lost to history. It is in the public domain because its copyright has expired. The original is in the collection of Britain's National Maritime Museum.

- The map of the route of the Spanish Armada was created by cartographer Frank Martini, History Department, United States Military Academy at West Point. It is in the public domain as a work of the US federal government.

- The 1885 illustration "Assasinat de Jumonville" is taken from the book *La Regence et Louis Quinze* by Alexandre Dumas. It is in the public domain because its copyright has expired.

- The photograph of Ontario Premier Mitchell Hepburn with the Dionne quintuplets is from Library and Archives Canada and is in the public domain because its copyright has expired.

- The photograph of the Hans Hollein sculpture of Volkswagens in Karlsruhe, Germany, was taken in 2011 by Michael Kauffmann. It is used here under the CC BY-SA 3.0 DE license.

- The photographs of Leonardo da Vinci's *The Last Supper* before and after restoration are in the public domain because the copyright of the original art has expired.

- The illustration by Lynn Johnston for her comic strip *For Better or For Worse* is covered under copyright and trademark. It is used here under "fair use" provisions of the copyright law to illustrate a biographical entry about the artist. Its resolution is too low to make it suitable for the production of counterfeit works and no comparable "free use" or public domain alternative exists.

- The 1973 photograph of Dame Thora Hird was taken by Allan Warren and is used here under the CC BY-SA 3.0 license.

- The oil painting of Ian Fleming, titled *For Your Eyes Only*, is by Constance Vlahoulis and is used here under the CC BY-SA 2.0 license.

- The 1961 MGM studio publicity photograph of Carroll Baker is in the public domain because it was published between 1923 and 1963 and its copyright, if any, was not renewed.

- The 1716 painting of King George I of Great Britain is by Sir Godfrey Kneller, Bt., and is in the National Portrait Gallery in London, England. It is in the public domain because its copyright has expired.

- The photograph of John Fogerty at the 2011 Cisco Ottawa Bluesfest was taken by Brennan Schnell and is used here under the CC BY-SA 2.0 license.

- The photograph of T-Bone Walker at the 1972 American Folk Blues Festival in Hamburg was taken by Heinrich Klaffs, and is used here under the CC BY-SA 2.0 license.

- The Goudey Sport Kings football card of Jim Thorpe is in the public domain because it was published between 1923 and 1963 and its copyright, if any, was not renewed.

- The 1859 engraving of Noah Webster, from the frontispiece of *Webster's American Dictionary of the English Language, Revised and Enlarged*, is in the public domain because its copyright has expired.

- The 1951 studio publicity photograph of Audie Murphy in *The Red Badge of Courage* is in the public domain because it was published between 1923 and 1977 without a copyright notice.

- The 1932 photograph of Edward VIII as Prince of Wales is from the German Federal Archives (Bundesarchiv), by Aktuelle-Bilder-Centrale, Georg Pahl (Bild 102-13538). It is used here under the CC BY-SA 3.0 DE license.

- The stamp engraving of Ezzard Charles was created by Czesław Słania, and is in the public domain.

- The photograph of an emerald was taken by Les Facettes and is used here under the CC BY-SA 3.0 license.

- The photograph of a lily of the valley (*convallaria majalis*) is by H. Zell and is used here under the CC BY-SA 3.0 license.

- The photograph of a hawthorn (*Crataegus monogyna*) is by Sannse and is used here under the CC BY-SA 3.0 license.

- The illustration of the month of May from *Hennessy Hours* is by Simon Bening, circa 1483/1484 — 1561. It is in the public domain because its copyright has expired.

- The political cartoon "On Decoration Day" is by John T. McCutcheon, collected in the 1905 book *The Mysterious Stranger and Other Cartoons by John T. McCutcheon*, published by McClure, Phillips & Co., New York. It is in the public domain because its copyright has expired.

- The photograph of the 1906 automobile calendar by Edward Penfield is from the Library of Congress Prints and Photographs Division, and is in the public domain because it was published prior to January 1, 1923.

- The 50-year perpetual calendar photograph is in the public domain.

License Description and Terms

Aside from material purely in the public domain, photographs and other material in this book are used under specific licenses permitting free use, usually with attribution. For full text and terms of these licenses, click or enter the appropriate links below.

- Creative Commons Attribution 2.0 Generic (CC BY 2.0): http://creativecommons.org/licenses/by/2.0/deed.en

- Creative Commons Attribution-Share Alike 3.0 Generic (CC BY-SA 3.0): http://creativecommons.org/licenses/by-sa/3.0/

- Creative Commons Attribution-Share Alike 2.5 Generic (CC BY-SA 2.5): http://creativecommons.org/licenses/by-sa/2.5/deed.en

- Creative Commons Attribution-Share Alike 2.0 Generic (CC BY-SA 2.0): http://creativecommons.org/licenses/by/2.0/deed.en http://creativecommons.org/publicdomain/zero/1.0/deed.en

- Creative Commons Attribution-Share Alike 1.0 Generic (CC BY-SA 1.0): http://creativecommons.org/licenses/by-sa/1.0/deed.en

- CC0 1.0 Universal (CC0 1.0) Public Domain Dedication (CC0 1.0)

- GNU Free Documentation License (GFDL): http://en.wikipedia.org/wiki/Wikipedia:Text_of_the_GNU_Free_Documentation_License

Timespinner
Press

www.ingramcontent.com/pod-product-compliance
Lightning Source LLC
Chambersburg PA
CBHW020902310526
45786CB00018B/1621